After dropping out of university and working as a pharmacy technician and a van driver, John Leach began training for the ministry at King's College London in 1976. He continued his studies and worked for a research degree at St John's College Durham, and was ordained priest in 1982. His first curacy was in an Anglo-Catholic market town parish in Norfolk, and from there he went to work with Canon Robert Warren at St Thomas' Crookes, Sheffield. He moved to be vicar of a parish in Coventry, where he stayed until becoming national director of Anglican Renewal Ministries in September 1997.

A musician and a liturgist, John is a member of the council of PRAXIS, a liturgical training organization, and of the Grove Worship Series editorial group (GROW). His publications include *Living Liturgy*, a practical guide to using liturgy in Spirit-led worship.

John is married to Chris, and they have three children. They live in Derby.

Leading Worship that Connects

A TRAINING COURSE

John Leach

First published in Great Britain in 1999 by
Anglican Renewal Ministries
4 Bramble Street, Derby DE1 1HU
and
Lynx Communications
Holy Trinity Church, Marylebone Road,
London NW1 4DU

British Library Cataloguing-in-Publication Data
A catalogue record for this book is available
from the British Library

ISBN 1 901443 17 5

Typeset by Wilmaset, Birkenhead, Wirral

Printed by Interprint, Malta

Contents

Introduction to the Course   1

The Structure of the Course   5

PART ONE - MAKING CONNECTIONS   11

Session 1   Connecting with God   11

Session 2   Connecting with Others   16

Session 3   Connecting with Different Age Groups   22

PART TWO - THE PROCESS OF LEADING WORSHIP   25

Session 4   The Backdrop   25

Session 5   The Planning Process   31

Session 6   Planning Liturgy and the 'Service of the Word'   41

Session 7   Preparing   49

Session 8   'Performing'   54

Session 9   Reviewing   61

Session 10 Growing   65

Recommended Background Reading   71

This book is dedicated to the people of
St James', Styvechale, Coventry with whom
I learnt and taught the following material

Introduction to the Course

Why another course?

The answer to this question is, quite simply, because more and more 'amateurs' are involved in the leading of worship in churches around the country. By 'amateurs' I mean, of course, those who have not been trained as 'professionals' at theological colleges or via courses, and don't get paid for leading worship; I don't mean to imply that 'amateurs' are any less good at the job. You already know that isn't true!

A national consultation on Lay Leadership of Worship by the liturgical training organization PRAXIS identified several areas of need for training, and this course is just one attempt to begin to meet those needs, particularly from a charismatic Anglican perspective.

Who is the course for?

The answer to this is: it is for those who find themselves 'up front' in a public act of worship in a leadership position, and want to fulfil their role more effectively, or for those who may want to explore a sense of calling to this ministry. Some clergy may want to expand the precious little training they are likely to have had during their preparation for ordination, at a college or on a course. This applies equally to Readers and their courses. Also, it is for those lay people who find themselves leading worship more and more. Similarly, a church, as a matter of policy, may want to train a team of leaders. An approaching interregnum or a new church plant may provide the opportunity to see people equipped for this new area of ministry, as might a pastoral reorganization that will leave decreased clergy availability.

Clearly, a call from God to be involved in any area of ministry needs to be made up of two parts – your call as an individual, and the church's recognition (or otherwise) of that personal call. One of the most disappointing things you can experience is to feel that God is calling you, but then to have that call 'turned down' by the church, usually by an incumbent who just doesn't feel, for all sorts of reasons, that this ministry is right for you. It's vital, therefore, that everyone understands right from the start that doing this course neither ties members into leading worship afterwards, nor the church to inviting them to do so. It is purely and simply a training course, and often having a go at doing the job, which this course entails, can show you, or your leaders, very clearly that this isn't right for you. So treat this course as an exploration rather than an immediate licence.

How is this course to be used?

This material has been used in two different ways in the past. Both have advantages and disadvantages. In a single local church that is training a new team, everyone is likely to share broadly common presuppositions and churchmanship. They will be working with a similar service pattern and ethos, and the same building(s). A lot of time can be saved by taking this common ground for granted. However, there is great richness to be found in working with a mixed group – for example, in a group of parishes or a deanery, or even an ecumenical grouping. As presuppositions are challenged and ideas broadened, a much greater feel for the area can emerge, and the worship practices of an individual church can be enriched by cross-fertilization with others.

A third possibility might be for you as an individual to pick up this book and teach yourself. It obviously won't work quite as well in this way: the group discussion sections, for example, might get a little monotonous! But if you ignore the rubrics and simply use the material in your own way, picking up from the teaching and thinking through some of the questions, and perhaps discussing them informally with friends or your incumbent, there will still be much to be gained. Since this is the least likely way that this course might be used, I won't include this possibility as an option in the text; you'll just have to use it as you think best.

The course is designed to be led not necessarily by a 'professional', but by someone with at least a little more experience 'up front'. In a local church this should ideally be the incumbent or someone delegated by them who leads, since it is important that in matters of style and churchmanship lay worship-leaders work happily under the authority of the whole church leadership. This course is not designed to train someone to become the leader of the opposition! However, it will work best if the leader is open to learn from the material too!

What's in this course?

The leading of an act of worship runs through five stages, and the course is based around them. We begin in our heads with the attitudes, theology and style we have adopted, maybe unconsciously. All this forms the *backdrop* against which we worship, but it would probably benefit from a rethink, so we begin there.

The next phase is *planning*, arguably the most important phase. An act of worship can stand or fall on things that have been done well or badly weeks before it starts. The *preparing* phase involves all we do just before the service to make sure we're absolutely ready.

Then there is what I will call '*performing*', although I'll keep the term safely inside inverted commas to remind us that worship is far from being a performance by the leader. I simply mean everything that happens during the course of the service itself.

Finally, there is the phase of *reviewing* afterwards how things went, a phase without which there will be no growth in our leading skills.

These are the main phases we'll be working through, but there are three other emphases that will colour the way we work through them. The first is about connecting with *God* as we worship, and how we might respond to an encounter with him. The second is about how we might connect with *other people* as we lead worship, and particularly with those who might be new to the church. User-friendliness will be a constant theme running through the course. And thirdly, the question of connecting with *different age groups* will also matter, since many of the services we are likely to lead will be all-age, at least in part.

Who is behind this course?

This course employs material used widely by me in several different parish and deanery settings over several years. I am now Director of Anglican Renewal Ministries (ARM), an organization that exists to encourage appropriate expressions of charismatic renewal within the Anglican Church in England. Before that I worked in three different parishes of varying churchmanship, but also exercised a training and teaching ministry over a much larger area. Material from this course was used in Coventry Diocese to train lay people for authorization in leading worship.

I am the author of several books on the area of worship. *Living Liturgy* (Eastbourne: Kingsway, 1997), my *magnum opus*, explores in greater depth many of the ideas discussed in the present book. While it is not essential that you should buy a copy, you will certainly find it helpful. I am a musician and liturgist, and I am a member of various national liturgical bodies.

Clearly, this material, published under the Anglican Renewal Ministries banner, will have a charismatic bias, but it is nevertheless intended to be useful in all sorts of different churches. Many of the principles it contains hold true whatever context we're working in, and where the charismatic bias does come out most clearly, it will be carefully argued rather than taken for granted.

The course will also be clearly Anglican, although there will be much that is of practical value to other churches, particularly those that have a liturgical element in their worship. It has been used successfully in different ecumenical settings, where participants were able to approach it with a willingness to learn from other traditions and reflect honestly on their own.

The Structure of the Course

Leading Worship that Connects is designed to be used over ten Sessions, each of approximately 90 minutes. The notes will assume weekly meetings, but you may of course meet fortnightly, or miss some weeks altogether for school half-terms or other essential interruptions. It might be possible to cram all the material into an intensive weekend, but this would mean that you miss out on the homework, as well as on time for reflection. Some ideas take root and grow slowly.

The course is split into two parts:

Part One looks at three emphases that will colour the way we look at the rest of the material:

1 Connecting with God

2 Connecting with others

3 Connecting with different age groups

Part Two explores the process of leading worship:

4 The backdrop

5 Planning

6 Liturgy and the 'Service of the Word'

7 Preparing

8 'Performing'

9 Reviewing

10 Growing

Each Session will consist of teaching, as well as practical exercises of different kinds. Some homework or background reading will be required of participants, but the whole idea is for the course to be fun.

It will deliberately build some sort of 'team feel' and camaraderie into the participants. This is to be encouraged, but beware of creating an élite group within the church.

Who should do the course?

The simplest scenario is that you are already a member of a group of people regularly leading worship, and would like to receive further training. But if in your church you want to train a team from scratch, things can be more difficult. Factors such as these might be important to your leadership in inviting people on to the course:

❖ Who has the spiritual stature already among the congregation? Who are the people who would automatically be nominated if you were to ask the congregation for suggestions?

❖ Who has begun to show the potential for leadership and for 'up-front' public positions?

❖ Who might be capable of doing the job, with all that it entails?

❖ Has anyone offered themselves for training? Is God putting this calling into people's hearts?

None of these factors is conclusive, of course, but, taken together, they might give your incumbent a sense of whom to invite. If you are doing the course in a way that involves more than one church (or denomination), it will obviously be up to the different church leaders involved to select their people.

A wise leader will also be looking out for those who might show potential for the job, even if they are very new and inexperienced as yet, and praying that God will call out from within them any gifting that at present lies dormant, but which is visible in potential.

How to use this manual

An outline for each Session will be given, which will include various different activities, including teaching from the leader(s). You will obviously need to make this your own, so as well as outlines I have included some illustrations from my experience that can be replaced with similar ones from your own. Obviously the leader will need to be at least half a step ahead of the rest of the group; therefore it is important to do some background reading well in advance so that there is an overall feel for the material. This will allow for its adaptation as necessary for the peculiarities of your situation!

All the normal skills and responsibilities of being in a group will be important: keep confidentiality within the group; don't let one or two people with a lot to say dominate the discussion; start and finish on time; and so on. There is already plenty of material on group dynamics and leadership in existence, so I'll take all that for granted.

I have tried to time each activity of a Session, as a guide rather than as a restrictive framework. Feel free to 'go with the flow' at times, but don't feel free to omit half the material or to finish at 2 a.m. because of bad timekeeping. The aim is to keep the Sessions sufficiently fast-moving to sustain interest, while dealing with the content in sufficient depth to be of real value.

You will need some bits and pieces of equipment for the course, and these will be listed at the start of each Session. For most of the course it will be useful for people to bring their own Bibles and notebooks and pens, to supplement this manual and to note down particular insights that come from the teaching or discussion. You will also need a flipchart or overhead projector on which to collect 'brainstorm' responses or to draw simple diagrams. Note now that for Session 6 you will need a few copies of *Patterns for Worship* (Church House Publishing, 1995). You will need at least one book for every six people, and preferably more, so begin to ask friends if you can borrow theirs for that evening if your church does not have several copies.

Some of the Sessions will work perfectly well in a home or church lounge, but for others it will be important for you to be, as far as possible, in the setting in which people will actually be leading worship. If more than one church is involved, it might be helpful to hold the Sessions in different places for different weeks.

Homework

Each member of the course will need a copy of this manual: photocopying is illegal except where permission is expressly given. As well as containing the notes for each group activity, it also provides for some work to be done between Sessions. This may take the form of background reading, devotional material, preparation for the next Session, and so on. Group members should be expected actually to do the work, which is by no means onerous, and a good leader will create a culture in the group activity slots where it is taken for granted that members have at least done some of the work required of them. Constant failure to keep up will not only rob members of much of the benefit of the course: it does not bode well for any worship-leading future, where planning and preparation are the keys to success.

A word on prayer

It is right that a course on leading worship should be done in the context of prayer and worship, and each Session will include a specific time for prayer, but I have kept to a minimum any instructions on how you might use that time. Creativity is needed by those responsible each week: it is all too easy to fall by default into an unstructured time of open prayer or a monologue by the leader. Matters such as the use of objects, music, pictures, liturgy and so on can make prayer times more interesting, as well as providing ideas for subsequent use by the trainees. A specific worship time could be delegated to different group members week by week – and of course it is not necessary to restrict prayer or worship to the times mentioned in the outline for each Session.

After the Session

One of my college tutors used to say (about a dozen times a week!), 'You don't learn from experience; you learn from reflecting on experience.' Reluctantly, I have come to agree with him! The notes for the early Sessions end with some questions to think through at the end of the evening, with a view to improving the functioning of the group. While these questions are particularly aimed at leaders, it is fine for group members to chip in with any comments that are helpful, as long as they are not meant to threaten or discourage, but to stimulate even better practice. When the questions stop, after Session 5, it doesn't mean that you can stop reviewing, just that you've got the idea by now!

Leaders might like to talk through these questions with another member of the group: this could be the most important function of a deputy or assistant leader. Personally, I prefer to do this immediately after the last group member has gone home, although others feel that a bit more distance from the events you're reflecting on is helpful. But don't leave it so long that the Session retreats into vague memories of a 'nice time'. It might be helpful to reflect over the phone the next day. Don't make this bit too heavy or detailed, or wallow in guilt and despair. If you feel you blew it, learn from it and move on!

Finally, it is worth saying that although I have written this course, I don't have a monopoly on worship-leading skills. There may be places where you need to adapt my material, or even disagree with it totally. That's fine, as long as you do so thoughtfully and not as the result of an immediate gut reaction. I may be wrong, but I do tend to be wrong *carefully*, so things against which you may instinctively react do have good reasons behind them: you should only reject them once you've *understood*, but disagreed with, those reasons.

So here we go! Enjoy it!

SESSION 1 Connecting with God

Aims

❖ To begin the gelling of the group.

❖ To become familiar with the course and the way it works.

❖ To begin to explore a theology of worship.

Leaders' background reading

Living Liturgy (Eastbourne: Kingsway, 1997), chapter 1.

Equipment

Enough copies of this manual for everyone.
Flipchart or overhead projector and pens.
Spare Bibles and pens/paper.

Outline

Welcome and introductions	*10 mins or 30 mins with coffee*
Group exercise	*5 + 10 mins*
Teaching	*10 mins*
Discussion	*15 mins*
Group exercise	*10 + 20 mins*
Prayer	*5 mins*
For next time	*5 mins*
Coffee (if not earlier)	

Welcome and introductions (if necessary)

If you're having coffee it might be a good idea for the first week to do so at the beginning as people gather, in which case allow 30 minutes. In subsequent weeks you could move this to the end or the middle of the Session as you wish.

The basic purpose of the course is to provide training and experience in leading others in public worship so that we can increase our skills and/or explore a possible calling into this ministry.

The leader should give out the manuals at the beginning of the Session.

Group exercise

Individually, identify the most memorable worship experience you've ever had. Then get into pairs and tell one other person about it, then listen to their experience. Try to identify any common factors both your experiences shared (both occurred while you were alone/both in cathedrals/both involved silence, etc.). [5 mins]

Collect on a flipchart any common factors the different pairs identified. [10 mins]

What did you find?

How many of these experiences happened at a normal Sunday service at your church?

How many mentioned, in different words, a sense of the presence of God?

What does all this tell you about the sort of factors which may make worship 'special' for people?

Teaching

What is worship?

Lots of people worship all sorts of things and people, in places as diverse as Wembley Stadium and mosques. Is there anything distinctive about Christian worship?

Read Exodus 33.1–3, 12–17.

The background to this is the Golden Calf incident, after which God was so angry that he would no longer go with the people on their journey, but would only send an angel instead (vv. 1–3). Note the people's distress at this (v. 4), and Moses' intercession. The key verses are vv. 16–17: if the presence of God is not with his people, how will anyone know they are special and different from every other worshipping community?

The distinctive thing about the worship of the living God is that he is present with his people, and can be encountered in that worship. The presence of Jesus on earth physically, and his gift of the Holy Spirit, is the Christian continuation of this Old Testament understanding of the presence of God. But it is now enriched because the

Jesus who became human is now in heaven, and still human. Jesus did not stop being a man at his Ascension, but continues as a man in heaven. Thus God is present with humanity, and humanity is present with God.

The aim of leading worship is to help people towards experiences like those identified earlier (in the Group Exercise) by facilitating an encounter with God.

Discussion

It is common practice in some circles to speak of God 'turning up' as we worship, and the use of the prayer 'Come Holy Spirit' is widespread. Is this a helpful way of speaking and praying? Is it scriptural? What might the dangers be? Do you agree with this passage from *Living Liturgy*?

> *It has been very popular in some circles over the last few years to speak in terms of God 'coming' or 'turning up' as we worship.*
>
> *I don't really have a problem with this understanding, and I [have] spent a lot of time building a whole theology of worship around it. I argued (and I still believe) that there is excellent biblical and liturgical evidence to suggest that 'Come, Holy Spirit' is a perfectly good prayer to pray.*
>
> *So it is not theologically or practically incorrect to speak of God coming. However, I have recently begun to question whether it is the best way to describe what we experience as we worship. I'm concerned, first of all, about the times when there aren't bodies littering the floor. If we talk positively about God's presence, it's quite difficult to avoid at such times at least thinking (even if we don't actually say anything) about his absence. Secondly, I would want to do everything I could to prevent Christians moving away from an understanding of worship as us entering humbly into God's presence: that's a great temptation when we think we can summon him into ours. He is not at our beck and call . . .*
>
> *But more importantly, I think we need to rediscover what it means to have a trinitarian understanding of worship. I don't mean by that that we need to make sure that all three of them get an equal amount of attention, but rather that the dynamic life and*

relationships of Father, Son and Spirit are reflected in the ways we talk about worship.

I believe [now] that it is more helpful to see the work of the Spirit in terms of catching us up to where God is than bringing God down to where we are ...: a trinitarian understanding of worship is more about us being carried into God's presence than him being called into ours.

Group exercise

What sorts of things might happen to us when we encounter God? Explore, perhaps in sub-groups of three or four, incidents from the Bible and from your own experience of meetings with God, and the difference they made long term. [10 mins]

Collect some of these suggestions on the flipchart. These are the kinds of things we want to see happening as we lead worship, and the course will help us to see them happening more and more. [20 mins]

Prayer

Pray for the course, and for each other, that God might teach us and anoint us for the ministry of worship-leading, so that others might be helped into life-changing encounters with God such as those we've already mentioned.

For next time

Think again about the idea of 'encountering' God. List the contexts in which you are already, or are likely to be, leading worship. Is it an All-age or Family Service? Evensong or Matins? An informal charismatic rave? A funeral?

Jot down what expectations you think the worshippers in your context(s) will have of encountering God, and what such an encounter might mean to them.

After the Session

The leader(s) should reflect on the following questions:

❖ Overall, how did you feel this Session went?

❖ Did the discussion flow, or were there lots of embarrassing silences?

- ❖ Did people seem to understand the teaching?
- ❖ How was the timekeeping?
- ❖ What would I 'rewind' and do differently?

SESSION 2 **Connecting with Others**

Aims

❖ To introduce the concept of 'user-friendliness'.

❖ To identify and learn from examples of bad practice.

Leaders' background reading

Living Liturgy (Eastbourne: Kingsway, 1997), chapter 4.

Equipment

Flipchart or overhead projector and pens.

Outline

Welcome and loose ends	*5 mins*
Group exercise	*5 + 10 mins*
Role play	*10 mins*
Teaching	*15 mins*
Brainstorm	*15 mins*
Teaching and discussion	*15 mins*
Prayer	*10 mins*
For next time	*5 mins*

Welcome and loose ends (from last week)

Any reactions to last week's material? Any bits which, on reflection, you found you didn't understand or agree with? The group may choose to allow some time for this if you feel the issues are important enough and are not covered elsewhere in the course.

On a flipchart, collect the worship-leading contexts you identified during the week (there may not be too many of these if you are a single-church group).

Group exercise

In this Session (in a similar vein to Session 1), identify individually any services you can remember that you feel were really *badly* led. Share

16

with one other person some of the things you felt the leader got wrong. (Try to avoid identifiable fiascos involving other members of the group!) [5 mins]

Collect on the flipchart some common errors identified by the pairs. [10 mins]

Role play

One member of the group (perhaps previously warned by the leader, and of fairly robust character) has invited some people (the rest of the group) to a Sunday service of their choosing, and quite naturally they want to know what they're likely to be in for. Unfortunately, the people who have been invited are all space aliens from the Planet Tharg, and while they are not unintelligent, and have a rudimentary grasp of the English language and simple concepts like 'sit', 'sing' and so on, they have no ecclesiastical background at all. While your 'volunteer' describes a typical service, the rest of the group are to be as obstructive as possible, with questions like, 'We do not understand: what is this "narthex" of which you speak?' (Try to avoid getting into deeper philosophical issues such as, 'What is this "God" of which you speak?': save that for your evangelism course.)

Teaching

The aim of this exercise is to help you to realize the extent to which the Christian culture is absolutely riddled with concepts and jargon that mean absolutely nothing to those outside the 'club', and the ease and frequency with which we relapse into the language of Zion – and thus alienate visitors.

This opens up another vital concept: that the worship-leader is not just there to relate to God. He or she must know how to handle the congregation properly.

Listed below are nine different roles in which a worship-leader might function. Look briefly at each one (no more than two minutes on each, less on some: just enough to grasp the concepts).

1 Host

Whenever people come together to worship – be it for a church service, a praise celebration, or a home meeting – there needs to be a host. People like to feel welcomed, in rather the same way as when you are a guest in someone's home. All good hosts know how to make people comfortable, and to feel that they count in that particular gathering just as much as the regular residents.

2 Figurehead

It is important, if worship is to be successful, that everyone feels secure – secure in God and secure in whoever is responsible for what is happening. So there needs to be someone present, whether or not they actually conduct the main body of the worship, who is seen by everyone as ultimately responsible for what is happening. And that person has to inspire confidence, both by their physical presence and by their sensitivity to the Spirit.

3 Articulator

By this term I mean someone who gives expression in words to what people are thinking and feeling. This will normally be near the beginning of the service, and the great value of speaking the right words here is that worshippers are drawn together into a common sense of the context of this particular time of worship. The words used may simply express how good it is to meet and praise God. Or they may be far more specific: 'We will all find it difficult to think of praising the Lord this morning after the tragic riots in our city last night. Events like these raise all sorts of questions for us, but we know only God can make any sense at all of the evil in our world. So let's offer him our praise.' The role of the articulator, then, is to understand the feelings people are bringing with them to worship, to gather them into corporate expression, and to help the congregation to worship with and through these feelings rather than to put them on one side or ignore them.

4 Leader

Every act of worship needs a leader, of course. The question is, 'What kind?' A true leader goes first into the fray, to encourage everyone else to follow. Yet some clergy, in particular, have a way of seeming to be above the battle – not part of the struggles that belong to everyone's life and therefore to their worship. It is so important that people should not be pushed or manipulated, but *led* into worship.

5 Encourager

So, as articulators we have expressed the common feeling, and as leaders we are setting the tone of worship. Yet some people would rather be elsewhere; it happens to all of us from time to time. We need encouragement: to be taken beyond our self-consciousness and inhibition. Those present for the first time will especially need the ministry of the encourager, but each one of us wants to be led into the experience of worship, not just once but repeatedly, as new depths of intimacy are found.

6 Protector

As people come to worship, they can be anxious and fearful – perhaps most of all in charismatic worship. At the back of their minds may be concern about false manifestation of gifts, demons needing to be confronted, disruption by disturbed people, the whole thing moving out of control. The congregation needs to feel protected from anything they conceive as potentially harmful, and the leader needs to give them this security.

7 Priest

The worship of God is a powerful thing. The Spirit may move us to tears or laughter; we may be strongly convicted of sin, or even fall down. The leader is priest as well as protector, and must understand the ways of God and of the Enemy (as well as of the human spirit when it is disturbed!), and show the spiritual discernment to help people know where to resist the Enemy and where to flow with what God is doing.

8 President

The Anglican liturgy uses this term for the celebrant at the eucharist. It is closely linked to the concept of 'priest'. Someone who presides at any kind of function is there to facilitate what people have gathered to do, and this makes the role of 'president' equally important for other services that are 'sacramental' (for example, weddings and funerals).

9 Prophet

A prophet is gifted to convey to people the heart of God. This may include speaking words of prophecy; in fact, it often does. But more than that, the prophet is called to act 'prophetically' throughout the time of worship.

Brainstorm

Using the contexts for worship-leading that you identified during the week, try to identify the kinds of people for whom they might be leading (newcomers, engaged couples in church to hear the reading of banns, elderly traditionalists, etc.). Which of the nine roles just listed might be particularly needed for some of these people groups?

Can you think of any other roles?

Teaching and discussion

Can you think of any times in worship when the leader has made you feel insecure? If so, this is almost certainly due to a lack of 'presence' on the part of the leader.

But what exactly is 'presence'? Brainstorm possible ideas towards a full description of this concept. Consider 'the ability to stand up in public without making the audience feel nervous for you'. Do you feel this is a good starter?

What sort of things might we do to increase our 'presence'?

Prayer

You have already identified different 'people groups' who might be the recipients of your potential skills. You could pray for them as groups, and/or you could pray for (and lay hands on?) each other, asking God to increase your anointing for the tasks of worship-leading.

For next time

Read Matthew 18.1–6, 19.13–14.

Jot down some thoughts on Jesus' attitude towards children. Why do you think he had this attitude?

After the Session

The leader(s) should reflect on:

❖ How the group is gelling.

❖ Whether people seem to be understanding the concepts.

❖ How comfortable you as a leader are feeling with the group and the material.

Are any changes of style needed at this stage?

Connecting with Different Age Groups

Aims

❖ To explore the various needs of different people in a worship context, particularly children.

❖ To raise awareness of the skills required in working with different age groups.

Leaders' background reading (recommended, not essential)

C. and J. Leach, *And For Your Children* (Crowborough: Monarch, 1994 – available only from ARM), chapter 11.

Equipment

Copies of Figure 1 'What Do We Need in Worship?' (p. 23), if possible photocopied up to A3 size.
Pens.
Flipchart or overhead projector and pens.

Outline

Prayer and worship	*15 mins*
Groupwork	*30 mins*
Discussion	*35 mins*
Summary	*5 mins*
For next time	*5 mins*

Prayer and worship

Read Psalm 103. How many different age groups are mentioned or implied in these well-known words? Thank God for each of them, and the contributions they can bring to worship.

Also bring into your praying some of the insights you gained by looking during the week at Jesus' attitude towards children.

Groupwork

Hand out the grids photocopied up to A3 size (failing this, people can use the ones in this book). The grid divides the human race into five age groups (pretty arbitrarily – there could be a lot more) and the different areas of need that they have: physical, mental and spiritual. In pairs, work on filling in as much as you can of the grid. For example, under 'elderly' and 'physical' you might write down the need to sit down after the first eight songs! The aim of this exercise is to help people think through imaginatively the needs of others.

Figure 1 What Do We Need in Worship?

	Babies and toddlers	Children	Youth	Adults	Elderly
Physical					
Mental: *Emotions*					
Mental: *Intellect*					
Mental: *Will*					
Spiritual					

Discussion

You may like to draw a much larger grid on several sheets of flipchart paper, and collect some of the needs identified by the pairs. Work a square at a time, rather than a pair at a time, and as you collect thoughts open it up for discussion. You may not get through all this in the time, and you will need to judge when people have had enough, but try not to omit one whole age group or one whole area of need.

End with some time on the wider implications of all this: what other groups are not identified, such as those with learning difficulties or disabilities? What might their needs be?

Summary

There is always the tendency when leading worship to regard the congregation as a monochrome block of people, but the groupwork and discussion has identified the vast spectrum of different people and needs. It is not easy to take all of them into consideration, but we need to try. The rest of the course will help us towards doing this.

For next time

Spend some time skim-reading the stories of Elijah (1 Kings 17—21, 2 Kings 1—2) and Elisha (1 Kings 19, 2 Kings 2—9)

Both Elijah and Elisha were powerful prophets, but they were very different in their *style*. List some of the differences.

After the Session

The leader(s) should think through the following questions:

❖ How well did people grasp the concepts involved in this Session?

❖ To what degree were they imaginative in thinking through the needs of others?

❖ How many marks out of ten would you give yourself/yourselves for the leading of the group?

❖ What might you have done to notch this up a grade or two?

SESSION 4 **The Backdrop**

Note for leaders

There are parts of this Session that you will need to handle differently depending on the composition of the group. If you are running the course with a group all from the same church, follow the parts marked 'Track A' where there is divergence. If you have a mixed group from different churches, follow 'Track B'. If you are from the same church, but from different parts (for example, some from a different congregation or church plant), you can choose either 'Track': read through the material and decide which you feel would be the most suitable.

Aim

❖ To identify and critique the values and styles that we have adopted (perhaps unconsciously) in our worship.

Equipment

Flipchart or overhead projector and pens.

Outline

Welcome and teaching	*10 mins*
Groupwork	*10 mins*
Discussion	*15 mins*
Groupwork	*10 + 10 mins*
Teaching	*5 mins*
Groupwork	*15 mins*
Prayer and worship	*10 mins*
For next week	*5 mins*

Welcome and teaching

A personal story from the author (*Leaders: feel free to substitute your own if it makes the same point*):

I was in the garden with a friend, wandering round, looking at plants and so on. We each had a mug of coffee: when I had almost finished mine, I flicked the last few dregs on to the garden.

'Why did you do that?' my friend asked.

'Because I always do.'

'But why?'

I thought for a while and then replied, 'Because my Dad always used to do it.'

This didn't sound very convincing, so I thought about it. I could picture myself in the garden at home, as a young child, and my father flicking the last few drops from his cup on to the garden. Why did he always do that? Then suddenly the penny dropped: it was long before the days of teabags, so, in spite of tea-strainers, the last little bit of his tea always contained a few tea leaves, which needed throwing away. So when in the garden (although not indoors, as far as I can remember) he would always flick them on to the ground.

Here was I, well into the teabag era, and drinking coffee, not tea, still doing the same thing for no good reason at all.

Sometimes there are things we do in our churches that are like that. There is the story of a church where the servers, when processing in at the beginning of the service, always did a little side-step at a particular point near the front. On enquiry, it turned out that 'that was where the lectern used to be' and they had to step round it, even though it had been moved out several decades ago.

Can you think of things in your church's life that are like that? Allow time to share stories for amusement or bewilderment.

The aim of this Session is to try to see the worship of our church(es) through new eyes, and to ask some questions about the way we do things and why.

We'll be looking at two things, *values* and *style*. Values are the things that are important to us, and style is about the way we do the things that we do. This will become more clear as we continue.

Groupwork

Split the group into up to five pairs or sub-groups. Assign the following shops, one to each pair/sub-group. If you have fewer than ten people, some pairs can have more than one shop.

The shops are:

Patel's Corner Shop
Tesco's
Fortnum and Mason
Aldi or Netto
Little Slurping Village Post Office

All of these shops sell food, but the way they do so reflects different values. In the small groups, try to identify the values each store holds.

Discussion

On a flipchart or overhead projector, collect the values each pairing or sub-group has come up with for each shop. Do other people agree that each pair/sub-group has correctly identified their particular shop's values?

Now talk about which is the *right* approach.

Is there a *right* approach?

If so, what makes it right?

What about churches? What values might different churches have? Are any of them right or wrong? Is it just a matter of personal taste as to whether or not a church:

    – uses incense?
    – has a choir or a worship team?
    – preaches biblically-based sermons?
    – is welcoming to visitors?
    – dresses its clergy up in robes?

Our values are often unarticulated, but are betrayed by what we actually do.

Groupwork

Track A

In groups of 5 to 6, try to articulate your church's values in worship. It may help to complete the sentence, 'Our worship at St Ethelburger's should be: ...', in no more than five bullet points. [10 mins]

Now feed back to the whole group and compare notes. Are there five agreed points? [10 mins]

Note: You may have a value and not yet be doing it, but it is valid so long as you're working towards it!

Track B
Split the group into sub-groups from the same churches. Each group should try to articulate their church's values in worship. If there are individuals on their own from one church, form a small group made up of these individuals from different churchs. It may help to complete the sentence: 'Our worship at St Ethelburger's should be: …', in no more than five bullet points. [10 mins]

Now feed back to the whole group and compare notes. Where are the contrasts and similarities? [10 mins]

Teaching

Style is much harder to get a grip on than *values*, but it is about the way we do things. It comes from our values, and can show us what they really are. For example, a church might say that one of its values is to be relaxed and informal, but in fact the vicar is quite staid and sober when there are a lot of older people in the congregation. This betrays the fact that one of his values is to keep the peace, and that that particular value overrides the stated one!

So what are our styles?

Groupwork

Track A
This exercise can be done as a whole group, up to a maximum of about 12 people, or subdivided if you have a larger number.

Track B
Stay in same-church groups.

Talk about all, some or one of these questions:
If your church was a meal, would it be:

❖ Sausage, egg and chips?

❖ Chicken vindaloo?

- Lobster thermidor au crevettes with walnut, roquefort and kiwi fruit sauce, endives and a vodka and elderberry coulis, served on a bed of wild rice with a fresh coriander and basil garnish?

- Ryvita and cottage cheese?

- Bean burgers, nut loaf, brown rice and fair trade coffee?

- Toad in the hole? Roast beef and Yorkshire pudding?

If your church was an animal, would it be:

- A little fluffy bunny?

- A man-eating tiger?

- A wise old owl?

- A Galapagos tortoise?

- A dolphin?

If your church was a newspaper or magazine, would it be:

- *The Daily Telegraph*?

- *The Little Slurping Advertiser and Gazette*?

- *The News of the World*?

- *The Journal of Ecclesiastical Law*?

- *Family Circle*?

Feel free to use your ingenuity to think up other sets of options!

If you've subdivided, and there's time, feed back some of your answers to the whole group. However, the real point is to help identify something of the style of the church(es), and to stimulate thinking about how we want to go about leading worship.

Prayer and worship

Read Matthew 10.1–4.

Although we don't know a lot about some of them, the disciples as a group reflected a huge diversity of personality and style. Reflect on how Jesus valued each of them, how he worked to knock off their rough edges, and how he used each in the work of his kingdom. Give

29

thanks for the diversity to be found in God's church, and (Track B) pray for each other's churches by name, for their leadership, people and ministry.

For next week

Complete *both* these sentences in not more than 50 words each:

1 'I think we should plan worship carefully because ...'
2 'I think we should be completely spontaneous when we worship because ...'

Can you find some Bible passages that back up each of these views? Which do you *really* believe?

After the Session

The leader(s) should review as usual:

❖ How do you feel you fared this week?

❖ How do you feel the people in the group fared?

❖ Is there anything you might have done better?

Are you beginning to get any feel yet for who might be showing great potential for worship-leading? Store this up in your heart for future reference.

SESSION 5 The Planning Process

Aims

❖ To learn that planning is not unspiritual, but vital.

❖ To introduce a model to help facilitate planning.

Note for leaders

The next few Sessions contain, of necessity, much more teaching, with less space for groupwork, than the earlier Sessions. The onus will fall on you to be happy and familiar with the material, but try to involve group members in discussion as you go along, rather than producing an hour's lecture. There are little questions put in from time to time that may stimulate discussion, although you will have to keep things moving along. If there is more than one leader, the sharing of teaching can provide a welcome change of voice and style.

Leaders' background reading

Living Liturgy (Eastbourne: Kingsway, 1997), pp. 111–30.

Equipment

Flipchart or overhead projector and pens.
Copies of the Alternative Service Book or the Common Worship Core Sunday book (or the Communion Service offprints of either) will be needed by each member for their homework.

Outline

Discussion and teaching	*40 mins*
Groupwork	*20 + 15 mins*
Prayer and worship	*10 mins*
For next week	*5 mins*

Discussion and teaching

Ask someone to read 2 Chronicles 5.12–14.

Now ask two more people to read out these quotes, both written about the same passage:

1   Sometimes, when we dare to let the Lord have his say, schedules and programmes have to be put away. 2 Chronicles 5.13–14 describes how when the glory of the Lord filled the house of God, those who were 'booked' to minister laid aside their ministry. Can you imagine it? All the work was finished. The house of the Lord was prepared. Choirs were rehearsed, trumpets were polished, 'the band' was ready ... the sermon for the grand opening had been sweated over for months, and then somebody started a chorus: 'The Lord is good and his mercy endureth for ever'. It took off! The place resounded with their united thanksgiving, and God inhabited their praise. He joined them. His glory filled the house.

    Be sure of this: when God really gets involved with the gathering of his people you may as well forget [what you've planned]. The King must do what the King must do!

2   Note that here, as in many other places in the Old Testament, free, exuberant worship does not exclude careful planning, preparation, direction and liturgy, but happens within a structured context (all is not lost for Anglicans after all!).

Which quote do you think best expresses the true meaning of the biblical text?

Which one do you resonate emotionally with more?

There is a view in some circles, and particularly in charismatic ones, that all planning and preparation is unspiritual: that it kills spontaneity and quenches the Spirit. While this obviously can be true, this course takes the view that it need not necessarily be so. In fact, planning is essential and can provide the best possible framework for spontaneity, as long as the possibility of flexibility is built in. So now we're going to learn how to do it!

We'll begin with principles, then look at three tools for the job, and finally we'll learn a method for the planning process.

The principles
A successful worship service should have four things, which we can understand by thinking of a pearl necklace.

Figure 2 Pearls of all shapes and sizes.

We begin with the raw materials, like a pile of pearls of different shapes and sizes lying on the table (Figure 2). What are some of the raw materials of worship? (Hymns, liturgy, silence, the collection, etc.) List as many different raw materials as you can on the flipchart.

2 Integrity

Figure 3 A string on which to hang your pearls.

So far so good, but now the idea is to find a string to hang them all on (Figure 3). This is the integrity of the service: what the service is about (baptism, the Christian's armour, harvest or whatever). This helps to hold the service together as a single unit.

3 Direction

Having got those two sorted out, you then need to begin to hang the pearls on the string in a particular and logical order (Figure 4). This gives the service its direction. You're starting somewhere, going somewhere, and even – hopefully – arriving.

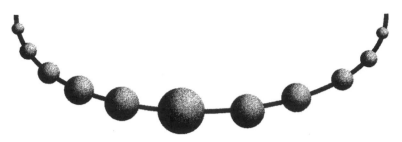

Figure 4 Stringing the pearls in a logical sequence.

4 Flow

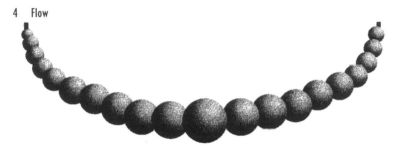

Figure 5 Creating a smooth and even flow.

Finally, the service needs to flow so that there are no nasty gaps or jarring moments, and the whole event feels smooth and logical (Figure 5).

Can you think of services you've been to that have violated these principles? Examples might be an unconnected string of events (many churches' attempts at *Songs of Praise* fall into this trap), or an aimless exploration of a theme (I once went to a service where every song, hymn and prayer had the word 'heart' in it, but for no apparent reason!).

The tools

Planning, like any other job, can be done more easily with the right tools. Here are three that can help:

1 A framework

Some kind of parameters can help you to know what can and can't fit into your service. Such parameters might be time (we must finish by midday; there's another funeral arriving in 20 minutes, etc.); they might be about the liturgical framework (we must fit Communion in somewhere; we must leave time for personal ministry). Obviously a firm grasp of the framework is essential.

2 A repertoire

This is a list of everything you might put into the service. It is particularly important with songs and hymns. Most of us use only a fraction of the 500+ hymns in our books and, with the charismatic music culture constantly churning out new worship songs, there is a need to decide which ones we use and which ones we won't use – however good these songs are, or however wonderful they sounded in the Big Top with 5,000 people joining in. This is based on the assumption that people can rarely meet God through music they're not familiar with. So draw up a list (50 hymns and 100 worship songs is adequate for most churches), update it annually, and refuse steadfastly to use anything not on it. If the song is *that* good, it will keep until your next revision, and it can be added then.

Liturgy works in a similar way, and the service books you have will provide a ready-made repertoire, although it can be much more helpful to introduce new material from time to time.

3 Categorization

It can be helpful to construct something like a topical index to save you from wading through the entire repertoire every time you want a song or hymn. Many books have a thematic index ('the cross', 'victory', etc.), but just as helpful is an index according to *feel* or *style*.

Six types can be readily identified (taken from *Living Liturgy* (Eastbourne: Kingsway, 1997), pp. 117ff):

(i) Adoration and love
This is perhaps the most intimate expression of worship. We simply stand before God, look him straight in the eye, and tell him that we love him. ...

(ii) Celebration and joy
This is a slightly less profound but much more exuberant form of worship, which might be described without undue irreverence as having a spiritual knees-up in the Lord's presence.

(iii) Proclamation and witness
Our hope as Christians is that quite apart from doing us good, worship can have an effect on those currently outside the kingdom. Sometimes we can design it specifically to do so. Many songs

announce the character and deeds of God, not just so that we can celebrate them but in order to draw others into an awareness of him.

(iv) Declaration and warfare
Sometimes we may feel in worship that instead of proclamation to people we have moved into declaration to the Enemy. Sometimes when we approach God in worship it's as if he invites us to come and stand where he stands, and then shows us the world or different situations through his eyes, as he sees them. This can often fill one not just with heartfelt compassion, but also with a real sense of outrage and righteous indignation.

(v) Intercession and penitence
These things have a place when we meet corporately, and indeed will become increasingly important as we move on in time. The element of sorrow and brokenness seems to have been restored to much contemporary charismatic worship. I see [this] as a real sign of the maturity of renewal ...

(vi) Teaching songs
Finally we recognise this category which, whilst not strictly speaking 'worship' nevertheless does have a place within our repertoire, and is especially important for children.

Can you identify some current hymns and songs in each category?

The process
How do we actually go about planning? We need to think our way through this checklist:

1 Context
What is the setting for this service/slot? We ask three questions:

(i) *Thematic context*
What is the service *about*? What are the readings, etc.? And what is the aim of the preaching/teaching? Who decides this?

(ii) *Liturgical context*
What is the setting of the service? Is it an Anglican Communion, a New Church rave, or what? Where does the bit we're planning fit into the overall shape of the service?

(iii) *Congregational context*

Who will be there, how many of them will there be, what ages are they, are they Christians used to this kind of worship, nominal churchgoers who only know 'Abide with me', or what?

2 Feel

What will it feel like to be there? What will the buzz in the air be? What has been going on for people that will affect them as they come to worship? How can we pick this up and take people with us?

3 Aim

If *feel* is about where people are now, where do we want them to be by the end? What do we think God might want to achieve through this service?

4 Flow

How will we get them from *feel* to *aim*? What is the journey we'll take them on, and where will we go on the way?

It's helpful to use a 'worship graph' to aid our thinking here. If you plot *exuberance* against *time*, you may get graphs that look like Figure 6.

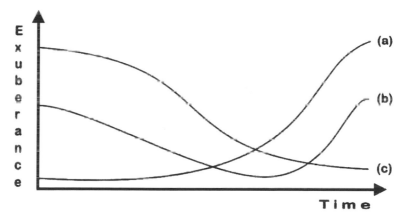

(a) Quiet worship, perhaps during the administration of communion, building to a joyful end to the service.
(b) An opening worship slot, beginning with celebration, moving into the penitential section, and lifting again as we know God's forgiveness.
(c) A lengthy and joyful celebration, moving gradually into intimate adoration.

Figure 6 Worship graph.

5 Content

Only after thinking through all these other stages can we begin to look at particular items themselves to see whether or not they fit. This is where the repertoire and its categorization comes in useful.

There is one final stage that is all too commonly missed out. Reviewing the service/slot afterwards is essential. This will be the subject for Session 9, so we'll leave it for now.

Groupwork

Divide into small groups of about 3 or 4, and allocate to each group one of the following tasks. You should think through the process and come up with at least the bare bones of a worship service or slot. [20 mins]

Each group should then feed back briefly to the whole group. [15 mins]

Plan some worship for:

Family Service on Gift Day

Your PCC has decided that you are going to give £10,000 to support the work of a Christian organization working with homeless people in Africa. The money will be given at your Family Service, at which Scouts, Brownies, etc. will be present. You have decided that the gifts will be brought forward in the context of a worship slot, following a reading from Exodus 25.1–9.

Outline the whole service, and plan the slot for the gifts.

Plan some worship for:

A Church Family Picnic

You have spent the afternoon together at a country park on a warm spring day, and you have passed the day playing games, looking for new flowers and buds, showing the children new-born lambs jumping around, and so on. You are now returning to the church for a brief service to round off the day.

Choose an appropriate theme, and outline a service.

Plan some worship for:

A Baptism Service

You'll have a church full of non-Christians for a baby's baptism, in the context of a Communion Service. The parents have been coming to church for a few weeks, and are beginning to know and enjoy your worship songs, but the vast hordes of their family and supporters are an unknown quantity. The vicar is determined to make the event thoroughly evangelistic, and has chosen Mark 10.13–27 as his reading. The children will go out at some point in the service, and will return during the Communion administration.

Plan the service, and begin to think about what music you might use.

Plan some worship for:

A Service of Morning Worship

About 50 or so people of all ages go to your church plant. You're preaching through St Luke's Gospel, and you're up to Luke 11:14–28. Normally, the children would go out, but you've just heard that your only children's worker is off with flu. There's no time to find a replacement, so you have to rewrite the service from scratch as an all-age event.

What will be the shape of the service, and how (apart from the sermon, which is someone else's problem) will you handle the theme?

Prayer and worship

As far as you can, use one of the group's suggestions to round off your evening.

For next week

Have a go at writing some liturgy. Choose one of the following tasks:

1 Write some responsive intercessions for a service to mark Guy Fawkes night. Include some congregational participation (but

'Lord, in your mercy, hear our prayer' is banned – no cribbing from existing liturgies!).

2   Sometimes in the Eucharistic Prayer in the Communion Service the president will slot in a 'Proper Preface' beginning, 'And now we give you thanks . . .' Have a look at some of the alternatives in the *Alternative Service Book*, pp. 154ff, or in the Common Worship Communion Service and write a couple of your own prefaces in the same format, for the Sunday when it is announced that your Gift Day total was £20,000 over target, and for a preaching series on the life of Abraham.

3   Look at the Collect for Purity at the beginning of the Communion Service: 'Almighty God, to whom all hearts are open . . .'. How might you write a different prayer for everyone to use at the start of the Communion Service?

Remember that good liturgy is biblical, poetic and easy to say!

After the Session

This Session involved a major teaching load for the leader(s), who should review as before:

❖ How well did it go?

❖ Did you feel on top of the material, and do you feel people grasped it well?

❖ Were you able to illustrate from your own experience?

SESSION 6 Planning Liturgy and the 'Service of the Word'

Aims

❖ To understand the value of liturgy in worship.

❖ To learn about the Anglican 'Service of the Word' and how to use it.

Equipment

Patterns for Worship (at least one copy for every six people – you may be able to borrow some copies if enough notice is given).

Outline

Debate	*5 + 15 mins*
Teaching	*20 mins*
Group exercise	*20 mins*
Feedback	*15 mins*
Prayer	*10 mins*
For next week	*5 mins*

Debate

What is this thing called 'liturgy'? Although virtually every church will be liturgical in that it will tend towards set patterns of doing things, particularly in worship, it will be helpful if we define liturgical worship simply as 'doing it from a book' – that is to say, following set and written forms of service, and expecting that for parts of the service the whole congregation will join in in saying and/or singing words previously written down for their use.

So is liturgy a 'good thing'? What do you think?

Read the following quotation from Arthur Wallis, one of the early pioneers of the House Church movement (taken from Arthur Wallis, *The Radical Christian* (Eastbourne: Kingsway, 1981), pp. 119f):

> *[Traditions] put a yoke on the neck of disciples, and especially on their corporate worship which produces bondage. Liturgies and*

fixed forms of service ... militate against our being able to
'worship by the Spirit of God'. Liturgies, whether ancient or
modern, written or unwritten, are a human device, to keep the
wheels turning by doing what is customary, rather than exercising
faith in the immediate presence and operation of the Spirit.
Consequently they cover up the need for the return of the Spirit
when he has departed, and they hinder faith for spontaneity and
variety.

Split the group into two halves, and hold a mini-debate on the motion 'This house believes that Arthur Wallis got it wrong about liturgy'. Each team is allowed about 5 minutes to decide on a main speaker, and to marshal their arguments before battle commences.

You could think about:

❖ Personal experiences, both good and bad, that make you agree/ disagree with Arthur Wallis.

❖ Whether liturgy is intrinsically good or bad.

❖ Whether the ways in which it is used and led are good or bad.

Note: In picking the two teams, the leader may find it helpful to ask any who are known to have difficulty with liturgy to speak *for* the motion, and vice versa. It can be good for you to have to put a point of view contrary to your own natural view.

Teaching

Note: Regardless of the outcome of the debate, we're going to learn how to use liturgy in this course. You should be aware in this section of any non-Anglicans in the group, but don't be apologetic: they've got a lot to learn about liturgy and it might just do them good!

Note for leaders

There follows now a huge wodge of material for the leader to present to the group. I have set it out as simply and concisely as I can, but you will need to make it your own, understand it fully, and teach it as creatively as possible. You can obviously include some discussion as you go along, but this information is essential for people to know, and in the end you'll have to tell them. Sorry!

The 'Service of the Word'

Because of the Anglican insistence on ordained priests celebrating Holy Communion, most of the services that people in the group will lead will be non-eucharistic (recap, if necessary, on the different contexts they identified earlier on the course).

The new Church of England way of dealing with non-eucharistic services is called the 'Service of the Word' (referred to as SoW from now on). This section is to explain the rationale behind this service, and how it is designed to be used.

A new approach to liturgy

What makes Anglican services Anglican? Until fairly recently, liturgists would have spoken in terms of 'common prayer', the idea (at least in theory) that every Anglican church would be using the same words in its worship, i.e. the 1662 *Book of Common Prayer*. However, over the past 20 years, with the proliferation of alternative books and texts, this no longer works – if in fact it ever did! So we have seen a significant shift to a different way of understanding what common prayer is. No longer do we see it as 'text'-based, but rather as 'shape'-based. In other words, it is the *structure and outline* of the service that is recognizable, rather than identical *contents*.

General Synod has recognized this formally by authorizing 'A Service of the Word', a unique liturgical authorization in that it doesn't contain one single word of text! Basically, it is a framework into which a whole variety of authorized texts can be fitted in a postmodern pick-n-mix way. It is to this service that many churches are moving, for All-age or Family Services, as a replacement for Morning or Evening Prayer, and even for previously unstructured charismatic 'celebrations' of one sort or another. It can also provide a framework for Baptisms and/or Thanksgivings and Confirmations if there is no Communion, and it may even form the first part of a Communion Service. So we need as potential leaders of this service to understand how it works, as well as understanding a few general principles of using liturgy.

Why authorization?

The Church of England believes that its doctrine (what it believes) is enshrined in its liturgy (how it worships). Therefore it takes great care that what we say in worship is actually what we believe, and will only authorize certain texts. It is of course acceptable to use some prayers from other books, and of course open or extempore prayer is to be welcomed, but 'core' texts such as creeds and, for some reason, absolutions, must be of the authorized variety. You simply cannot have each local church writing its own liturgy all the time, because it would in effect be writing its own doctrine. Anyway, there's so much in *Patterns for Worship* (see p. 7) that it'll be a very long time before you get fed up and need to look wider.

The framework

The legal framework of the service is simple: you need *The Preparation* (or the *Gathering Together*), *The Liturgy of the Word*, *The Prayers*, and an *Ending* or *Conclusion*. So the outline service looks like this:

Gathering Together

1 A liturgical greeting
2 Prayers of penitence
3 Praise – canticle, hymn, songs, etc.
4 The Collect of the day

The Liturgy of the Word

5 Bible reading(s)
6 A psalm or song(s)
7 A sermon
8 A creed or affirmation of faith

The Prayers

9 Intercessions and thanksgivings
10 The Lord's prayer

11 A liturgical ending

How does it work?

The resource book that makes it all happen is called *Patterns for Worship* (referred to as *PfW* from now on). This contains the outline, resource options for slotting into each section, and commentaries and examples of how a service might be put together. Once you get to know it, it's easy enough to navigate around it. *PfW* is also available on computer disk, and it is fairly easy to produce a service sheet if you choose to go down that route.

There are other books specifically designed and authorized for use in Anglican services, and material from them can be used within the SoW. *Lent, Holy Week and Easter* and *The Promise of his Glory* (containing material for use during Advent and Christmas) are two examples. In addition, other written prayers, which need not be specifically authorized, may be included.

So how do I plan a service?

Work through the process from last week, and then, in the 'content' section, choose some of the options that might be more appropriate, bearing in mind both the theme of the service and the people who are likely to be there. So if there are children present for all or part of the service, choose wisely to help them. And, if one option seems to fit the theme better, go for that one. Be aware, too, of the time of year, and follow the usual liturgical conventions of a more penitent feel during Advent and Lent, with a greater emphasis on celebration around the major festivals.

Presentation

The optional material is of two types: material that the leader can say that the congregation do not need to have in front of them, and material that is for them to join in with. The first type (e.g. introductions to the Peace, Confession or Lord's Prayer) is not a problem: you just use it. The second is more difficult. You will need as a church to have a policy on how people know what they're supposed to be saying.

Three methods of presentation have become popular. The first, made easier now texts are available on disk, is to produce a complete printed service each week, with everything there: liturgy, songs, hymns, even notices.

Another way is to build up a set of services for different uses and different seasons. The Communion Service for Lent, for example, may be printed in a small booklet with a seasonally mauve cover. This may give more attention to creative wording for the penitential section.

Another booklet, differently colour-coded, may be brought out for All-age services. Such service booklets often include only the bare essentials. The parts said by ministers and leaders are omitted, and the congregation simply have before them the words in which they join, and cues to bring them in.

The third, more radical way is to dispense with books and put everything up on overhead projector slides or 'Power Point'. This has the advantage that no one needs to fiddle with books and finding things. But a disadvantage is that children may find it more difficult than reading from something in their hand. The following passage is taken from *Living Liturgy* (Eastbourne: Kingsway, 1997), pp. 142–3.

In a book, the things you've just finished saying are still there, and if you want to you can peep ahead and look at what you're going to be saying soon. But when your liturgy is projected onto the wall, only the current, present piece of text is available. Past and future have no way of making themselves present other than through memory.

You may not feel that this is a major disadvantage, but it does mean that to stay with a particular line which has spoken to you, is made very difficult, particularly, as is often the case, if the line or word which has hit you is one which you have not really noticed before, and of which you therefore have no memory. Similarly the link between what you do in church on Sunday and what you do at home during the week is weakened. So I personally am less keen on OHP liturgy, although it does have its uses for the occasional special item or in addition to text printed in the book . . .

Beware!

All these different options are marvellous and can alleviate boredom, but if we overdo it people will feel they're coming to a completely new event each time, which rather defeats the whole object of being liturgical. So make sure there is some material that is used on a pretty regular basis.

Doing it

PfW is very keen on action as well as words, something we can easily miss out in a non-eucharistic service, so try to fit in something for the congregation to do: sharing the Peace, for example, or creative ways of conducting the prayers that might involve the congregation more than we normally do at Communion Services. We'll go into this more later on in the course.

Music

There are points when it is particularly appropriate to sing, but feel free to put music in at different places. Two important principles: the opening hymn or song(s) should help us gather together and should be 'big' and well known, and the very last event of a service is not a hymn or song; it is the ending or dismissal. The use of hymns or songs to leave to should be discouraged. It would be good for the church to rediscover the Psalms: although they can be replaced with songs, don't do it too much. How about saying a psalm that then launches into singing?

Group exercise

Split into sub-groups of no more than six, with a copy of *PfW* for each group. The task for each group is to produce a short Service of the Word using next Sunday's theme.

You will need to be told what the theme and readings will be, and what sort of congregation is expected. The aim of this exercise is to help you become familiar with *PfW*, not to produce a stunning act of worship, and the leader(s) may need to move around the groups doing a bit of coaching. (Leaders will, of course, need to have already become fairly familiar with *PfW* themselves!)

Feedback

Each group should talk the rest through their service, explaining why they have chosen the options they have. Be critically constructive with one another, particularly with regard to the pearls from last week: does the service have integrity, direction and flow?

Prayer

Share briefly your homework, and your attempts to write liturgy. Did you find it easy? In the light of that, what do you feel about liturgists who write material for the church? Spend some time praying for them, and especially the Liturgical Commission and its members.

You may also like to use part of one of your services, bearing in mind the difficulties of not having texts in front of you.

For next week

 Postman Pat is about to go out for his day's rounds in Greendale. Make a list of as many things as you can that he will have to remember to take with him (van keys, Jess, trousers, etc.).

Aims

❖ To teach how to be absolutely ready to lead the worship you've prepared.

❖ To help spiritual preparation as well as practical preparation.

Equipment

Flipchart or overhead projector and pens.

Bibles.

Gentle music for meditation and something to play it on.

Outline

Group discussion	*10 mins*
Teaching	*20 mins*
Bible study	*20 mins*
Teaching	*10 mins*
Meditation and prayer	*25 mins*
For next time	*5 mins*

Group discussion

Brainstorm and collect on the flipchart people's ideas on *everything* that Postman Pat will have to remember to take with him on his rounds (letters, van keys, trousers, etc.).

What would happen if he forgot some of these items?

The aim of this is to show that without attention to minute detail, disasters can happen.

Now brainstorm what service leaders might need to have ready as they go out to begin a service. Make as long a list as you can.

Teaching

Some random hints for making sure you're prepared (please add any of your own):

❖ Arrive in good time before the service starts. Ideally, allow 30 to 15 minutes before 'take off' to arrange your books etc., 15 to five minutes for relaxing, liaising with others, last-minute panics and so on, and five to zero minutes for praying with other people involved in the service. Try to be in position on the dot of the starting time, and time your departure from the vestry accordingly.

❖ Before you go out, think your way through each part of the service in order, asking yourself what books etc. you'll need, which page you'll need them open at, and so on. If this is done carefully, you'll have everything to hand during the service itself, thus avoiding gaps that are nerve-racking for you and distracting for the congregation.

❖ Know your own limitations: if you have eyesight difficulties, photocopy and blow up texts you need so that you can read them without having to hold the book in front of your face. You can also cut and paste (on a computer or with scissors and glue) lots of different bits to save undue page-turning (although you need to remember to allow the congregation time to turn *their* pages).

❖ Prepare for yourself a 'master sheet' with the full outline of the service, page and hymn numbers, reminders about posture, etc.

❖ Don't write out a full script for 'rubrics' (things you say to introduce or announce liturgical texts or music), because people will be able to tell very quickly that they are being read to. But do make notes to remind you of the thread of thought that holds the service together, and that will affect the way you introduce and link items.

❖ If you do something wrong, turn it into a laugh. This will warm the congregation to you, rather than annoying them (provided, of course, you don't do it too often!), release tension for you, and relax the congregation. Don't be seen to be panicking, and *never* apologize in advance for anything: that immediately tells the congregation it won't be very good, and even if it *does* turn out to be OK, it'll be much harder to convince them that it was! Brim with confidence, even if it means faking it.

❖ Remember all the age groups we talked about in Session 3. Remind yourself constantly by looking around the congregation as you speak, and consciously noticing the children, the elderly, and so on.

❖ Smile a lot.

Bible study

Read Zechariah 3.1–7.

Although not primarily about leading worship, this passage contains a picture of what it often feels like as we go out to lead worship. We suddenly become aware of how sinful and unworthy we are, we may well have had a row at home before we left, and we feel like making a bolt for it rather than processing reverently into church! If you haven't already had this experience, it won't be long before you do!

What can this passage teach us about this?

Who is behind the guilt we feel? (The Hebrew *Satan* means 'accuser'.)

Why do you think he likes to make us feel guilty?

Why especially before we go to lead worship?

What does Joshua have to do to get free?

What does he have to do to stay free?

Teaching

Two brief but extremely helpful bits of teaching:

1 Conviction and condemnation

It is vital we learn to tell the difference between these two:

Condemnation	Conviction
The work of the Enemy:	*The work of the Spirit:*
to point out general weaknesses,	to point out specific sins,
so that we can feel bad,	so that we can let God deal with them,
so that we're left feeling separated from God,	so that fellowship with God can be restored,
and unworthy to do anything for him.	and we can minister confidently.

A good way of dealing with this, when we're feeling got at, is to ask the question, 'What have I done wrong?' The Spirit will tell us, specifically, times and places, but the Enemy will say vague things like, 'Well, you're just useless, all the time!' Listen to the Spirit and co-operate with him, but resist the Devil and he'll run from you.

2 Anointing and role

Sometimes we'll go out front feeling full of the Spirit, ten feet tall and ready for anything. The Lord is really with us in power, and great things may happen during the service. This is wonderful, and to be welcomed, but what about the other times, when we feel nothing at all, or worse?

It is true in ministry that sometimes we will function under the powerful anointing of God, but at other times we will function not 'under anointing' but 'in role'. In other words, God will honour and use us because of the role we have at the time, the role that 'the church' has bestowed on us, that of service leader. I'm not sure you can prove this from the Bible, but it certainly seems to work in real life! Some of my most powerful times of ministry and leadership have been when I've felt the *least* close to God or full of the Spirit.

None of this is an excuse for neglecting our relationship with God, but it is meant to teach that we minister first and foremost through grace. To believe that God will only use us when we feel good, or when we have managed to work up enough devotion, is at best legalism and at worst superstition. First of all, we're loved and accepted, then we serve God: it's never the other way round.

Meditation and prayer

You may like to have some gentle background music on during this meditation. Read, slowly, Luke 3.21–23a, then lead a meditation along the following lines:

> *'You are my son, whom I love; with you I am well pleased.' These words are spoken again by the Father later on during Jesus' ministry, on the mountain of Transfiguration. They make sense there: Jesus has been faithfully serving his Father for some time, and there is much for the Father to be pleased about.*
>
> *But at his baptism? What has he done to deserve this favour? He is about to start his ministry: up till then all he has done is make a few coffee tables and wardrobes. How can the Father say he is pleased with him? And how can our heavenly Father be pleased with us when we have done so little, so falteringly, so ineffectually, for him?*
>
> *The answer is that the Father is pleased with his Son simply because he is his Son – in the same way that he is pleased with us*

simply because we are his sons and daughters. Just as those of us who have children love them because they are our children, regardless of whether or not they please us by what they do.

Jesus told his disciples that they were no longer servants, but friends. Relationship comes first, service later. We seek to please God because he first loved us: we do not seek to serve him in order that he might love us.

Picture yourself going down slowly into the water of baptism. See the dirt of guilt and the enemy's accusation floating off you and drifting off downstream. Feel the water cleansing, healing and refreshing. Now receive the Holy Spirit, filling you with love for Jesus and empowering you for ministry. And hear the Father saying to you, personally, 'You are my son, you are my daughter, whom I love. With you I am well pleased!' Receive those words; receive that truth into your mind; reject as coming from the Enemy any hesitation to accept the truth, any tendency to exclude yourself or see yourself as a special case to whom that doesn't apply.

Now give thanks to God for his love for you, and his confidence in you. Rejoice, not because of the great things you might achieve for him, but because he has chosen, loved and accepted you, and promised you a place with him in heaven for ever.

Now encourage people to speak out prayers thanking God for this truth and for his love and grace.

Note: There may well be people in the group for whom this meditation is very powerful, negatively or positively. Be prepared to cope with tears or other strong reactions. Be aware, in particular, of those whose parenting and/or church background has taught them a graceless and legalistic Christianity, those for whom the idea of free acceptance seems too easy or too liberal. You may have some pastoral work to do during the week!

For next time

It will really help you in the next Session if you can have read chapters 8 and 9 of *Living Liturgy* (Eastbourne: Kingsway, 1997) before you start. Try to get hold of a copy (you can even buy your own – it's bound to come in handy later!) and read through the chapters in preparation for having a go yourself next time.

SESSION 8 'Performing'

Aims

❖ To allow each member of the group to have a go at leading some worship.

❖ To 'earth' what we have learnt so far in constructive criticism of others' attempts.

❖ To allow the leader to see people in action, and to gain some idea of their skills.

Equipment

Various service books, hymn books, etc.

Outline

Group activity	*75 mins*
Prayer	*10 mins*
For next time	*5 mins*

Notes on this Session

This Session sounds the most terrifying one, but is also the most enjoyable and rewarding one, believe it or not! The basic idea is that each person uses what they've learnt to lead a part of a service, while the others use what *they've* learnt to be as critical as possible.

This Session should, if at all possible, be held in the actual place where some or all of the group will be leading public worship, rather than in someone's house or a church hall or room.

By this stage, the group should have gelled nicely, so there should be no threat in this exercise, but it is worth making the point at the beginning that we're saying what we're saying out of love and concern for the person and those whom they are leading, and not out of a desire to be nasty. Anyway, once you realize that the rule is that the critic is the next to have a go, you become a lot less critical – in my experience anyway!

The whole evening is spent on this activity, and it should be kept as fast-moving, encouraging and light-hearted as possible: this provides the best environment for learning. This is arguably the most helpful Session of the course, as well as being the most demanding.

The rest of the group not 'performing' at any given time provide the congregation as well as the panel of jurors, and should join in where appropriate with prayers or other items being led by the one on trial.

The following notes contain several different aspects of a service. The leader should invite someone to have a go at one of them, and then invite comments about how they fared. The notes include the sort of areas to be watching out for: in particular, you should keep reminding one another of the chart from Session 3 at the beginning of the course and the needs of different people. *Living Liturgy* will give you lots of practical hints: you will need ideally to have read at least chapters 8 and 9 before the session.

I The welcome

Ask someone to welcome the congregation at the start of a service.

Watch for:

❖ Introducing themselves – who is this person leading the service, if not the vicar?

❖ Microphone technique (if appropriate)

❖ The warmth of their personality and the genuineness of their welcome

❖ Lack of jargon

❖ Lack of the 'cringe factor'

❖ Volume and clarity of voice

❖ Fidgeting or visible nervousness

❖ Practical hints – what to do if your child needs the loo, etc.!

(At first people may want to be too nice, so a few gentle questions from the leader such as, 'How well could you hear her?' or 'Do you think you'd know what a "sidesman" was if you were a first-time visitor?' might help people to sharpen up their critical faculties.

Follow-up questions like 'How might she have said that a bit more clearly?' will help the exercise to feel positive rather than negative.)

After two or three people have tried, summarize what you've learnt, and move on to the next item.

2 The notices

Ask your next victim to give out an imaginary set of notices for the week.

Watch for:

* Clarity of information – what do I actually have to do if I want to go to the event mentioned?

* Exclusiveness – how are visitors supposed to know who Mabel with the tickets is?

* Jargon – where is this 'narthex' where coffee is served?

* Brevity and conciseness

* Waffle – this part of the service is one of the few unscripted and often unprepared parts

* Hesitation, repetition and deviation!

3 Announcing a hymn or song

Watch for:

* The right balance between a curt 'Hymn 247' and a ten-minute sermon about what a lovely hymn it is

* Any clue as to *why* this hymn has been chosen for this point in the service

* Posture indications – these should come last, not first, in what they say

* Which book of the many available *is* 'Ancient and Modern'?

* The 'cringe factor': 'We want to see all you banns couples joining in the actions'!

4 Beginning some liturgical prayer

Pick a prayer that everyone will have copies of, or will know by heart (for example, the Collect for Purity), and get someone to lead the rest in praying it.

Watch for:

❖ Book and page numbers announced clearly

❖ Time given for them to find the page

❖ Why we're saying it: what we're supposed to be doing/thinking as we pray

❖ The actual synchronizing of voices at the start

❖ The pace and volume of the leader during the rest of the prayer

5 Announcing and ending a Bible reading

Get someone to announce and read a short paragraph, and then use the liturgical ending.

Watch for:

❖ Appropriateness of the introduction: if the church has pew Bibles, are people expected to be following the reading in them?

❖ If so: page number, reference, etc.

❖ Enough time to find it (especially for children)

❖ Clarity and volume in reading

❖ The ending: clear and strong, suitable pauses

6 Introducing a ministry time

The sermon is over, and now you want people to respond. Get someone to handle this response and lead into ministry in a way appropriate to your setting.

Watch for:

❖ Clear explanation

❖ Explanation for newcomers who won't have seen anything like this before

❖ Appropriate response categories

❖ Is the leader clearly confident, or do they themselves look terrified of the Spirit's activity?

7 Dealing with a prophetic gift or tongue and interpretation

Someone from the rest of the congregation should improvise and speak out a made-up word or picture from the Lord. They can decide whether to make it a helpful word, a word of knowledge for someone, a false prophecy, or merely a bland platitude. How is the leader going to deal with it?

Watch for:

❖ Confidence in dealing with it – not getting thrown off balance by it

❖ Appropriateness of response

❖ Clear instructions if a specific response is required

❖ Respect and non-embarrassment for people who may want or need to respond

Note: There may be opportunity for the leader to give some teaching here (briefly). The following hints might be helpful.

Prophetic words or pictures need to be tested, first by the person who thinks that they are getting something: 'Lord, if this is not from you, please take it away.' Second, by the church (most of the time through the leadership).

❖ Who is the prophet? Is she or he someone we know and trust?

❖ Is it scriptural? Does the Bible teach the same thing as this particular word or picture?

❖ Is it positive? Or is it just nasty and destructive with no 'door of hope' left for people?

❖ Is it right, does it fit in with the flow of the service or does it cut across it in a way that does not seem to make sense?

❖ Is it anointed? Does it feel as if it has the power of God behind it, or is it just a bland truism?

Similar questions need to be asked about tongues and interpretations, and the gift of discernment is essential for deciding whether other so-called manifestations of the Spirit (including some fairly bizarre behaviour during ministry times) are divinely inspired. Is this really from God, from the Enemy or from disturbed human personalities?

Generally speaking it is good to:

- ❖ Reinforce something which you feel genuinely does come from the Lord, for example by repeating the gist of the prophetic word into the microphone so that all can hear it clearly.

- ❖ Ignore that which is bland and lacks power.

- ❖ Publicly counter anything that you perceive to be evil and harmful.

8 Ending the service

Get someone to finish off the service in whatever way is customary for you: invitation to receive ministry, coffee, or whatever, followed by the Grace.

Watch for:

- ❖ Clarity of instructions

- ❖ Expectation of a further response of some kind, and how to do this

All this should take you most of the evening, but feel free to include any other aspects of service leading that may be appropriate to you. Remember too to think about style and how it varies in different contexts: the jolly approach at a Family Service may need tempering slightly at a 1662 Evensong or a funeral! I don't believe, however, that the contents vary that much: you still need to give clear and audible instructions at Evensong! And remember: there may well be visitors at services other than your main Sunday morning one.

Prayer

The evening will have been nerve-racking, tremendous fun, and probably the most important piece of learning of the entire course. Pray for one another for God's encouragement, for his turning of anything that was a bit hurtful into a helpful piece of learning, and for his further anointing for leadership.

Note for leaders

It is not uncommon that this Session will identify clearly to you as leader not just those who are 'naturals' at worship-leading, but also some people who simply haven't got what it takes. This is useful information for you to have at this stage, before people are let loose in public, but sadly it is beyond the scope of this course to tell you how to deal with them pastorally, other than as a reminder that people are happiest, and most fulfilled, and that the quality of the church's life is highest, when people are working within the gifting and anointing that God has given them!

For next time

The leader should choose two people to do a role play during the next Session. The aim of this is to role play a debriefing session and to handle it as badly as possible. The leader will know by now who might cope with this the best: he/she might be one of the people doing the role play, or they might both be group members. Basically, you need to ad lib a feedback session after an imaginary service, and the other person's job is to be as nasty and destructive as possible, leaving the service-leader a gibbering wreck at the end. If it is done well this should be tremendous fun to watch, and at least you'll know that nothing that ever happens to you could be that bad! The two people chosen should spend some time getting this ready before the next Session: the rest of the group should pray fervently for the victim!

Reviewing

Aims

❖ To teach the importance of review for growth in any area.

❖ To help towards structures that provide a forum for this review.

Equipment

Bibles.

Outline

Group discussion	5 + 10 *mins*
Bible study	15 *mins*
Teaching	15 *mins*
Role play	5 *mins*
Group discussion	20 *mins*
Prayer	15 *mins*
For next time	5 *mins*

Preparation: You will have had to prepare for the role play in advance of the Session, inviting the participant(s) and thinking through a rough outline.

Group discussion

Divide the group into pairs, and talk about last week and your reflection on it:

❖ Did you find it enjoyable?

❖ Which bits did you find hardest?

❖ Was there any criticism of you personally that you found helpful?

❖ Were there any criticisms that you found hard or hurtful?

❖ Can you identify one thing that you felt was really significant for you in growing in your skills? [5 mins]

Open this discussion up to the whole group to share your reactions to last week. [10 mins]

Bible study

Read Luke 10.17–24 and Matthew 17.14–21.

The background to these stories is that we have two glimpses of Jesus and his disciples 'debriefing' after ministry experiences.

❖ Why was it important for them to do this?

❖ What do you think they learnt from each of these examples?

❖ How do you think it felt for them to talk about their experiences?

❖ Do you think they acted differently after this as a result of these debriefings?

The aim of this study is to show that we learn from reflecting on experience, and that to fail to reflect means that we can easily carry on blindly making the same mistakes over and over again. It can be a vulnerable and, at times, painful experience, but we need to live with that. However, we need to debrief in as positive way as we can with the aim of encouraging rather than destroying each other.

Teaching

One system for reflecting on experience that has been found helpful and that doesn't proliferate unnecessary meetings is a system of 'Feedback Partners'. This section sets out the rationale and rules for this system, but if you have a better one, feel free to work with that instead.

How 'Feedback Partners' work:

1 When anyone is on the rota to lead a service, they take the initiative to invite someone to be their Feedback Partner for that service.

2 The Partner should be someone who has done this course, so that they know what they're looking for, and obviously someone who is going to be present at the service.

3 The Partner's job during the service is to 'take notes' (probably not writing them down at the time!) on the leader's 'performance', along the lines of last week's exercise.

4 They should note down the positives as well as the negatives, and aim to be as encouraging as possible, while not being afraid to confront any mistakes lovingly but head-on.

5 After the service, at a mutually arranged time, they should get together for a debriefing session of no more than 30 minutes. This could be face to face or over the phone, immediately after the service or later in the week, but no later than six days after the event.

6 The Session should begin with the leader reflecting on his or her own experiences, good and bad, and then move on to comments from the Partner. They should then pray together over any issues raised in the session.

7 That relationship is then over: the Partnership lasts for that one service only. Beware of people choosing the same Partner every time: a selection of different people will avoid mutual blindspots.

Note: The question of whether clergy as 'professional' leaders should be involved in some kind of a Feedback Partnership is an important one. It would probably do most of us no harm at all, but the practicalities of the sheer number of services we lead would make it pretty impossible to do according to the rules above. Perhaps the best way is to be seen to be inviting constructive criticism from time to time, perhaps for some special service or event.

The leader should make sure the group understand the rules, and are happy to enter into a contract to use the system. He/she may need to let the group know that they'll 'police' it to make sure it actually happens. It is good practice for the incumbent, when asking someone to lead a service, to ask also who their Partner is going to be, and when they intend to hold the debriefing.

The leader (or incumbent) will also need to negotiate with the group about further slots for the whole team for ongoing training and review, and of course pastoral relationships with the members will give ready access for feedback and encouragement of them.

Role play

The two people chosen last week should hold their barbaric debriefing session. Try to make it snappy: it will be difficult to sustain the joke for more than about five minutes.

Group discussion

After the role play is over, draw out in general discussion the important issues with questions such as:

❖ Was the criticism of the particular bit valid?

❖ How might the person have said this more positively?

❖ Was it really necessary for the person to have mentioned this particular point?

❖ What was the proportion of encouragement versus negative criticism?

And so on. The aim is to help you to acquire some of the skills needed in successful reviewing, and to learn to be positive and encouraging even when you have to slate your victim into the ground!

Prayer

You could use this time to pray for encouragement for one another. One way to do this is to form small groups of three. One of the three receives prayer, perhaps with laying on of hands, while the other two ask God to give them words, Bible verses, pictures or whatever to encourage them and build them up. Each person has a turn receiving prayer and ministry from the other two.

For next time

You will need, if at all possible, to get hold of a recording of the Vaughan Williams 'Coronation' arrangement of the 'Old Hundredth' ('All people that on earth do dwell'). Make sure you get the 1953 hymn version and not the 1928 setting of the psalm. It is readily available on various collections of choral music. Has anyone got it? If not, a friendly local choirmaster, or perhaps your local cathedral, should be able to help. You'll also need something to play it on.

Think through some recent acts of worship you've been a part of, and try to identify any particular *moments* that had a special impact for you. Write some brief notes about the service as a whole and the nature of the special time within it.

SESSION 10 Growing

Aims

❖ To empasize the importance of growing in any area of ministry.

❖ To discover how to work on continual improvement of our worship and our worship-leading skills.

Note: As the final Session of the course, this evening provides the opportunity for the tying up of any loose ends from the rest of the course. The programme should be flexible enough to allow time for any important and significant issues to be aired thoroughly, but should not be frittered away on more trivial issues that can be dealt with more simply. The leader will need to exercise judgement about this. Spare time is lost or gained in the prayer and ministry session at the end.

Equipment

A recording of Vaughan Williams's 'Coronation' arrangement of 'All people that on earth do dwell'.
Cassette/CD player to play it on.
If you have a piano or keyboard in the room, and someone who can play it, that would help too. If you can't get the Vaughan Williams music on record, cassette or CD, can you get the music for this musician to play?
Overhead projector or flipchart and pens.

Outline

Group discussion	*5 to 20 mins*
Teaching	*20 mins*
Group discussion	*20 + 20 mins*
Prayer and ministry	*10 to 25 mins*

Group discussion

This is the last chance to raise any questions from the rest of the course. Does anyone have any:

❖ Questions?

❖ Ideas you want clarifying?

❖ Concepts you've found it hard to agree with?

❖ Areas you don't feel have been covered?

The leader should allow time for any of these where you feel the discussion will benefit the whole group, and promise to talk one-to-one about any others not covered at this time.

Teaching

Share briefly any special moments that you identified during the week.

If you have managed to get hold of it, play your recording of the 'Old Hundredth'. Did anything happen to people as they listened to verse 5 (the final verse)? If so, was it at any specific point during this verse?

(Typically, there will be a range of reactions from nothing whatsoever to powerful physical tingles down the spine occurring on the word 'Ghost' at the end of line 1. For the technically/musically minded, this is due to the expected resolution to the tonic (G) being replaced unexpectedly with a move to the submediant major (E), and is known to psychologists as 'expectancy violation'. Due to some not fully understood mechanism, this causes a release of chemicals called endorphins in the brain which are responsible for the physical *frisson*.)

The point of this musical interlude is to illustrate the fact that for most people there is a sense of thrill or excitement when something unexpected happens. There is a lot we can learn from this about worship and worship-leading.

The effect of the unexpected E chord was, for some people, to make the whole thing more interesting and exciting to experience.

Would it have had the same effect if Vaughan Williams had used it in verse 1?

Would it have worked as well if he had done something different in each verse from 1 to 4?

What would have happened if he had gone to an E♭ chord rather than E? (If you have a pianist and a keyboard available, you could illustrate this for the group.)

The point of this rather esoteric discussion is to illustrate the following facts:

❖ The whole point of 'expectancy violation' is that the music leads you to expect something, but then violates that expectancy by doing something different. We needed the 'normal' harmonization in verses 1 to 4 so that we expected verse 5 to be the same. To have used it in verse 1 before any expectation was set up, or to have done something different each time so that no discernible pattern was apparent, would have severely limited the effects.

❖ The E chord, although not expected, does actually work: it contains the melody note B, as the G would have done. The E♭ chord doesn't work in the same way, and just sounds 'wrong', as any non-musician would be able to tell you.

❖ Another illustration of the way expectancy violation works is via a joke. The telling of the story sets up an expectation; the punchline violates it with humorous effect. Consider the following example of the genre:

A man is doing a charity parachute jump. During his brief training, the instructor tells him what to do:

'When you leave the plane, count to five slowly and pull the red handle. Your parachute will open and you will float safely to the ground. It won't happen, of course, but if there is a problem with the chute, don't worry, just pull this blue handle here, and the emergency chute will open. You can steer by pulling the ropes to your right and left: aim for the big white cross on the ground. When you land, there'll be a van with a nice hot cup of coffee to warm you up.'

So the man goes up in the plane, jumps out at the required height, counts to five, and pulls the red handle. Absolutely nothing happens. He panics briefly, but then remembers the blue handle. He gives it a yank, but again nothing happens. As he is plummeting at ever-increasing speed towards the ground, he thinks to himself, 'I bet there won't be any coffee for me down there either!'

It's the unexpected nature of the punchline that has its effect: if *we* were there, that's the last thing we'd be likely to be worrying about, although there is a certain logic to it.

Another example is the 'Englishman, Scotsman and Irishman' joke in its many manifestations. In the format that these jokes take, the first two men do much the same thing, but the third does something radically different and, hopefully, amusing.

(You may like to pause here for a time of sharing of people's favourite examples of the genre.)

This provides a picture of worship, and particularly liturgy. From the musical and joke illustrations, we can draw out the following principles:

❖ Worship that contains no 'surprises', and can therefore be termed 'predictable', will do a lot less for people than something that contains some different or unexpected elements. A G chord or a parachutist splatted on the runway would have had less of an impact (come to think of it, maybe not in the case of the parachutist!).

❖ For the 'surprise' to work, it must come within a familiar framework. If everything is different each week, there is nothing for it to be different from. Too many surprises cease to be surprising, and just become messy and irritating.

❖ The 'surprise' element must work: it must not be totally alien and unrelated to what has been going on beforehand. An E♭ chord or a parachutist suddenly turning into a rhinoceros would be surreal, not funny.

Group discussion

Return briefly to the 'special moments' you identified earlier. Does this insight help to explain any of them? (This isn't the only factor, of course, in making worship interesting!)

In the light of these principles, what might we do to create worship that is more creative and exciting? In small sub-groups, talk about some of the things that could make our worship more special. How could we avoid the 'overkill' effect that would rob unpredictability of its impact? [20 mins]

Feed back ideas to the whole group for their evaluation. [20 mins]
In case people get stuck, here are some practical ideas:

❖ Use of a song to replace a familiar piece of liturgy (*We Believe* instead of the Creed; *Tell out my Soul* replacing the *Magnificat*).

❖ Recorded music, with parts of the liturgy done as voice-overs.

❖ Visual images on the overhead projector during intercessions.

❖ Occasional use of incense and candles in a church that doesn't normally use them.

❖ Replacement of a familiar text once in a while with an equivalent from *Patterns for Worship*.

❖ A song from the Worship Team for people to listen to rather than join in with.

❖ Use of different symbols: at an ARM conference on Youth Ministry we began with a liturgy of lament for the young people who had left the churches of our nation during the last 20 years. We had one small seed for each of them, and poured them out on to the altar, all 907,000 of them, or 38 milk-bottles full. The impact of this act was far greater than simply telling people the statistics.

❖ Use of unusual music: a friend's funeral, a solemn and stately affair in Durham Cathedral, ended unexpectedly, but perfectly, with a recording of Edith Piaf singing *Je ne regrette rien*!

Not many of these ideas are radically new, but they are probably under-used (although beware of over-use!). But more important is learning to think in a way that is constantly asking, 'How can we make this special?'

The Danish philosopher Søren Kierkegaard said that the church has managed to do something even greater than its Lord: it has managed to turn wine into water. What an indictment on us that people regard the worship of the living God by his church as boring! We need to work with all the creativity we can get from the Holy Spirit to make our worship vibrant and alive, not just for the sake of visitors and newcomers, but because our God deserves nothing less.

Prayer and ministry

Pray for the Lord's anointing of creativity for each other, asking the Holy Spirit to come and fill each person with a new love for Jesus, new skills in leading his people into God's presence, and new creativity for the task.

Recommended Background Reading

J. Leach, *Living Liturgy* (Eastbourne: Kingsway, 1997).

J. and C. Leach, *And For Your Children* (Crowborough: Monarch, 1994).

M. Earey, *Leading Worship* (Cambridge: Grove, 1999) – as well as many other titles within the Grove Worship series on different aspects of worship leading.

Patterns for Worship (London: Church House Publishing, 1995). At the time of writing we are expecting an updated edition of *Patterns for Worship* within the next couple of years. The 1989 edition is now out of date and not recommended for this course.

Lent, Holy Week, Easter: Services and Prayers (London: Church House Publishing, 1984, 1986).

The Promise of His Glory (London: Church House Publishing, 1990, 1991).

Although the above three are primarily liturgical texts, the introductions and 'coaching tips' contained within them provide some very useful principles for this course.

J. King, *Leading Worship* (Eastbourne: Kingsway, 1988).

S. Townend, *Playing the Keyboard in Worship* (Eastbourne: Kingsway, 1993).

Although these are both musical technique books, they provide some tremendous insights into the leading of renewal worship. Don't be put off by the titles!

J. Leach, *Hymns and Spiritual Songs* (Cambridge: Grove, 1995) explains the difference between hymns and worship songs so that they may be used appropriately in worship.

J. Leach, *Responding to Preaching* (Cambridge: Grove, 1997) helps think through how people might respond to God and how we might help them to do so within a liturgical context.

Some older classics on worship leading within a charismatic context (NB: these are not desperately Anglican!):

G. Kendrick, *Worship* (Eastbourne: Kingsway, 1984).

D. Fellingham, *Worship Restored* (Eastbourne: Kingsway, 1987).

J. Lebon, *How to Understand Liturgy* (ET London: SCM, 1987).